A really large oinker...

ENTER: 2159

 × twenty

 + seven

 × fourteen

 =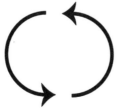

Scratching the chalkboard is one way to get the…

ENTER: .163

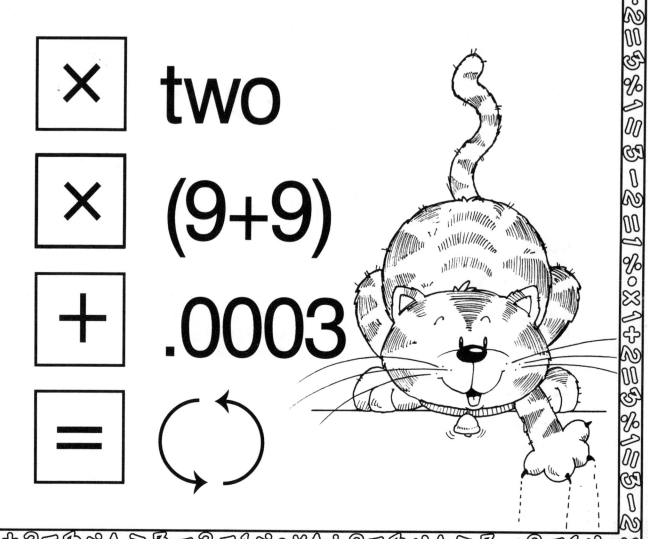

×	two
×	(9+9)
+	.0003
=	↻

Babies have to be fed very carefully when they are . . .

ENTER: 173

 160

 nine

 × 200

 + eighteen

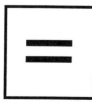 =

Some musicians play music to _____ to.

ENTER: 2...

☒ ×	three
☒ ×	fifty-six
☒ ×	nine
=	↻

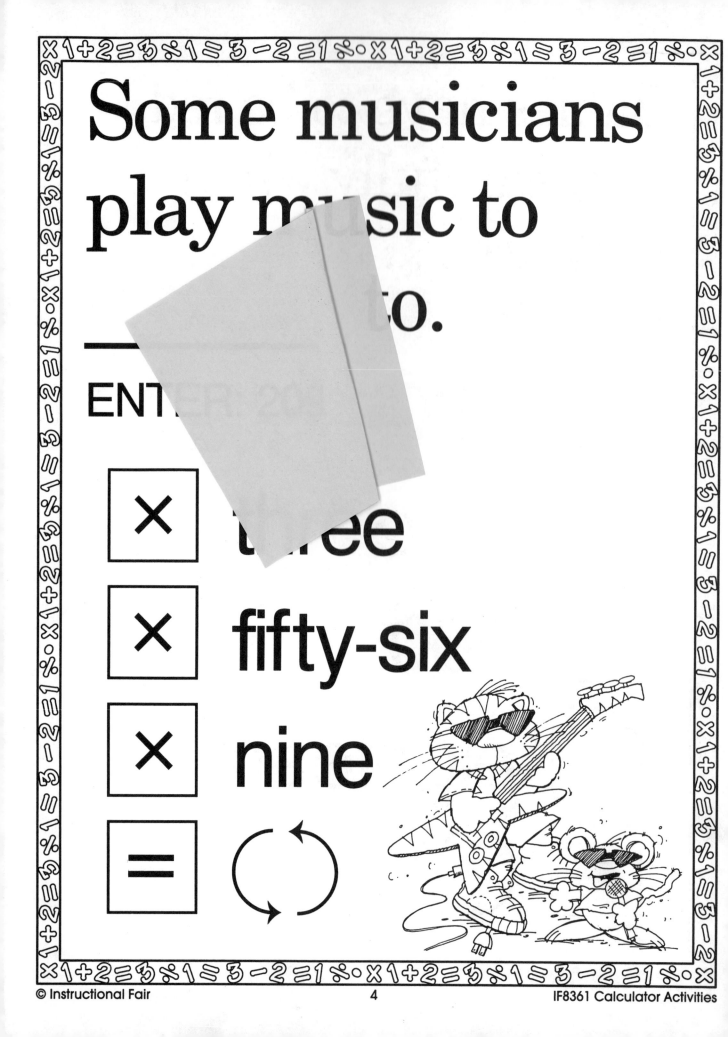

The name for a beautiful southern girl...

ENTER: 377

 × 100

 + thirty

 add (4+4)

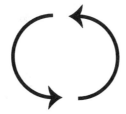 = ↻

Fish use _____ to breathe...

ENTER: 412

 × five

 × seven

 add nine

 × four

 =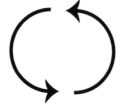

Playing the piano and building model planes are two great...

ENTER: 443

 thirty

 seven

 400

 four

 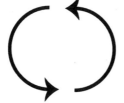

If there are no globs in your soup, then your soup is...

ENTER: 443

×	5000
+	123
×	twenty-five
+	one
=	↻

This girl's name starts and ends with "e"…

ENTER: 650

 54

 seven

 ten

 three

 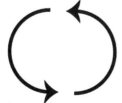

A baby bird will first need to peck out of its…

ENTER: 746

×	240
×	eight
+	seven
×	54
+	five
=	↻

Having a best friend is true...

ENTER: 788

 35

 nine

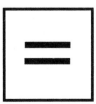 two

 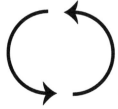

Add this suffix to "ishka" to make a word to tickle your tongue...

ENTER: 947

 multiply (the yard line in the center of a football field)

 × 8

 add (9+9)

 =

Telephone poles are made from...

ENTER: 934

×	five
+	three
×	four
×	fifty
+	three
×	six
=	

IF8361 Calculator Activities

What every dog dreams of being...

ENTER: 1000

 × the number of months in a year

 × three

 − 993

 =

A watermelon as large as a bath-tub is a real...

ENTER: 1583

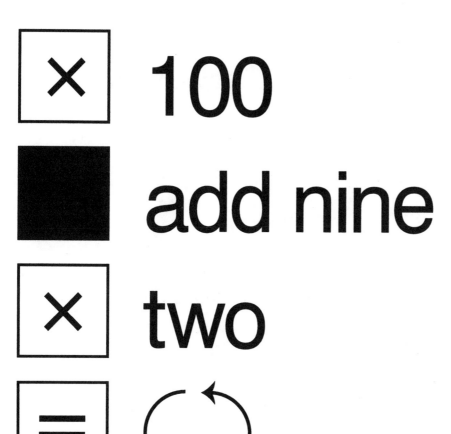

✕	100
◼	add nine
✕	two
=	↻

IF8361 Calculator Activities

Is it a boy's name or a beak?...

ENTER: 100

 **×**   three less than eighty

   add the number of pennies in two dimes

   subtract the number of ears on a dog

 **=**   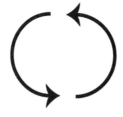

This African bird's beak looks almost like a shoe…

ENTER: 3859

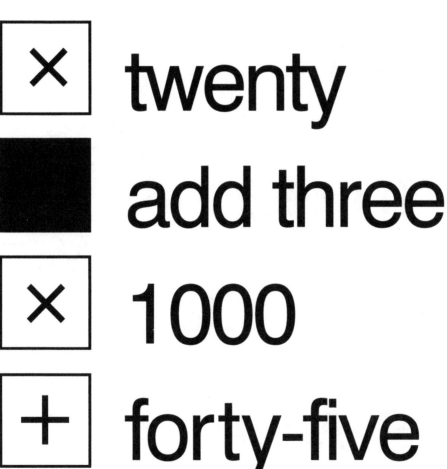

× twenty

■ add three

× 1000

+ forty-five

= ↻

Neat handwriting is...

ENTER: 4727

 80

 three

 ten

 seven

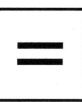 

Messy eaters need a . . .

ENTER: 8,000

	two
÷	two
+	ninety-three
×	200
+	(9 + 9)
=	↻

An empty beehive is . . .

ENTER: 13843

 200

 sixty-nine

 two

The polished table had a...

ENTER: 56.2

 × twenty

 × seven

 × seven

 = ⟳

A lump on the head …

ENTER: 61421

$\times$	ten
$+$	three
$\times$	108
$+$	two
$=$	↻

What you get when you fall down...

ENTER: 1000000

 × five

 + 8000

 add (2 x 4)

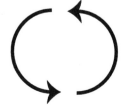 = ↻

Your tire makes this sound when you ride over a nail…

ENTER: 11111111

 two

Some rides at a fair can make you ...

ENTER: 1 x 1

 **add ten**

 seventy

 one

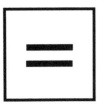 

On a walk down a seashore you might find many beautiful...

ENTER: one less than five

 5773

 twenty-five

 forty-five

 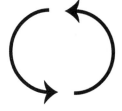

Something kids like to do…

ENTER: ten less than 100

 523

 seven

 eight

Flowers you might see at Easter are...

ENTER: the number after ninety-nine

| ✕ | 5317 |
| add ten |
| add seven |
| = | ↻ |

There is a poem titled "Three _____ Goats Gruff"...

ENTER: the only odd number: 2, 6, 4, 5

✕	70.6
✕	50
■	add one
✕	eighteen
=	↻

When you can't quite catch the baseball you might _____ it.

ENTER: the even number between 3 and 5

+	1890
×	twenty-five
▮	add one
×	eight
=	↻

A company symbol is called its...

ENTER THE EVEN NUMBER: 3, 5, 9, 7, 2

$+$	eight
$\div$	ten
$-$	.393
$=$	

Six in Spanish...

ENTER THE MISSING NUMBER:

10, 20, _____ , 40

 subtract the amount in five nickels

 204

 seven

 five

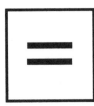 

The best place to lean on a window…

ENTER: the missing number:

43, _____, 45

 five

 seven

 **add three**

 five

 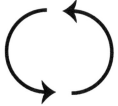

The contraction for "she is"...

ENTER: 13-9

−	two
+	three
×	1.069
=	↻

When you have lots and lots, you have...

ENTER: 10-5

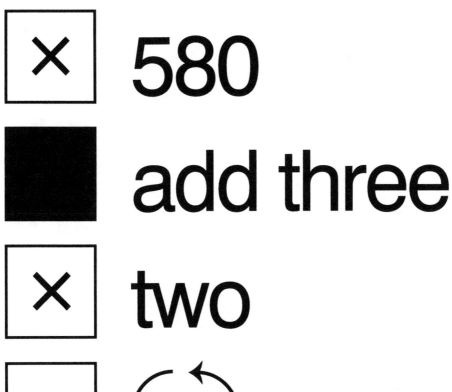

$\times$ 580

 add three

$\times$ two

= ↻

A nickname for Elizabeth...

ENTER: the next number...2, 4, 6, __

 add (6+6)

 five

 93

 thirty-one

 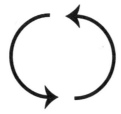

A word that means, "What did you say?"...

ENTER: the next number: 2, 4, 6, _

 two

 (5 + 5)

 60

 three

 $\circlearrowright$

Another name for "Oswald"…

ENTER: the next number in order…5, 10, 15, ___

■ Add (8+2)

■ Add (2+3)

☐ × 892

☐ =

When you can't stop laughing, you have a bad case of the…

ENTER: 50 + 50

×	531
+	seventy-seven
×	100
■	add fifteen
=	↻

A really high laugh sounds like...

ENTER: 10 + 10 + 10 + 10

 600

 119

 fourteen

Another name for cat...

ENTER: 20 less than 100

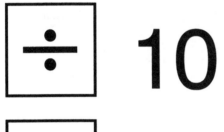 ÷ 10

 × 100

 + sixteen

 =

Turkeys do this all day long without taking a bite...

ENTER: two less than ten

 the number of days in a week not counting Saturday and Sunday

 7970

 six

The story of David and Goliath is in the . . .

ENTER: two less than ten

×	500
×	ten
−	2182
=	

What is the difference between a Chihuahua and a Huskie?...

ENTER: ten less than fifty

 eighty

 seventeen

 two

Let's go "dashing through the snow in a one horse open ___"

ENTER: five less than fifty

 eighty-two

 the number of people it takes to ride a unicycle

 **125**

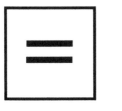 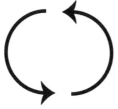

Hungry dogs prefer to hide their bones in their…

ENTER: one less than sixty

 **900**

+ **seventy-seven**

 **100**

+ **thirty-eight**

=

A girl's name with two *l*'s and two *e*'s...

ENTER: half of 1,000

×	640
−	63
−	2400
=	

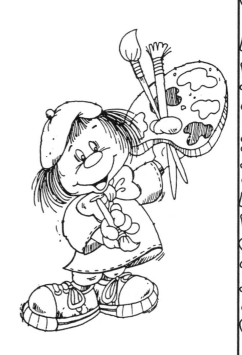

The speed at which a computer thinks _____ your mind.

ENTER: the smallest 3-digit number

×	eight
×	210
+	nineteen
×	thirty-two
=	↻

The first name of someone who lost her sheep?...

ENTER: the number of letters in "baa"

−	two
+	6.2
÷	nine
=	

The Spanish word for "bear" is...

ENTER: the number of letters in "bear"

÷ one

− four

+ .50

When animals get thorns in their paws they…

ENTER: the number of letters in "ocean"

 eighty

 947

 four

The first thing we usually say when we understand something...

ENTER: the number of letters in "mouse"

 six

 thirty

 twenty

This belongs with "Old MacDonald's farm"...

ENTER: the number of letters in "Moo Moo"

+	four
−	nine
−	.8687
=	

This connects to a fire hydrant...

ENTER: the number of letters in "yellow"

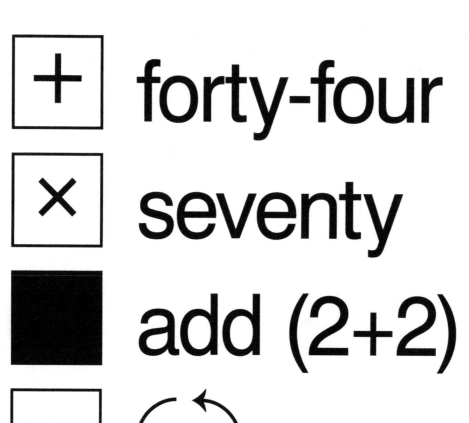

+	forty-four
×	seventy
■	add (2+2)
=	↺

Very light brown is...

ENTER: the number of letters in "magenta"

 add 2 + 3

 two

 6023

=

A one-letter word that is always capitalized . . .

ENTER: the number of letters in the word "capital"

+	eight
÷	three
-	four
=	↻

When you put too much peanut butter and jelly between your bread, it _____ out!

ENTER: the number of letters in "Mississippi"

 + twenty-two

 + 100

 × 400

= ↻

This state has a city named after the famous explorer Columbus…

ENTER: the number of syllables in "explorer"

 four

 twelve

 .140

To move up and down in water…

ENTER: the number word that sounds the same as "for"

$\times$	twenty-five
$+$	one
$\times$	eight
$=$	↻

Another word for "Golly"...

ENTER: the number that sounds like the past tense of "eat"

 the number of days in a school week

 two

 eight

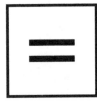 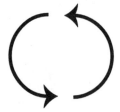

What you might say if your dog grabs your hamburger…

ENTER: the number of pennies in a nickel

÷	**five**
−	**.75952**
÷	**six**
=	

Bicycle chains need . . .

ENTER: the number of pennies in a dime

 × **fourteen**

 + **two**

 × **five**

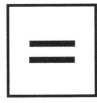 

George Washington said "I shall not tell a…"

ENTER: the number of pennies in a quarter

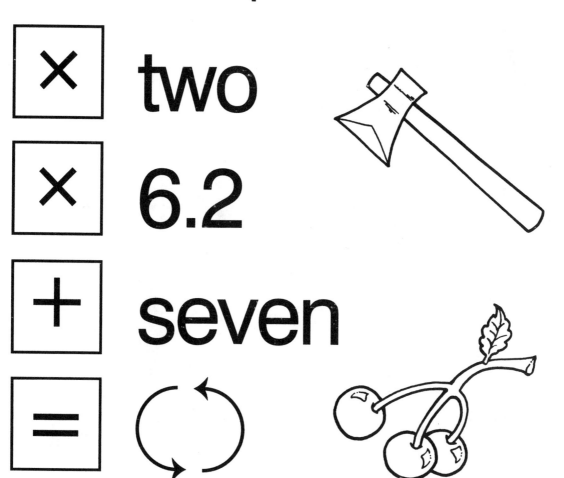

×	two
×	6.2
+	seven
=	↻

The bottom of your shoe…

ENTER: the number of pennies that equals one quarter

$+$	fifteen
$+$	$(2+2+2+2+2)$
$\times$	74.1
$=$	$\circlearrowright$

A nickname for Gilbert...

ENTER: the value of six nickels

 add 5.8

 five

 four

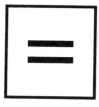 

Another name for a sister...

ENTER: the value of two dimes and a nickel

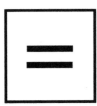 subtract ten

 ÷ three

 × 103

 =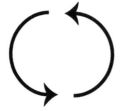

The person who gives orders is the...

ENTER: the number of pennies in one dollar

$+$	two
$\times$	three
$\times$	eighteen
$=$	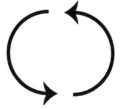

Some of the hardest working animals around...

ENTER: the number of cents in a half dollar

 **+** **five**

 **×** **100**

 **−** **162**

 **=** ↻

The Spanish word "hola" means...

ENTER: the number of quarters in a dollar

 ✕   two hundred thirty-two

 ÷   fifty-eight

 −   15.2266

 =   

Another name for a pig is a...

ENTER: the number of pennies in a dollar

✕	**six**
+	**ten**
−	**six**
=	

A large hermit crab's home is a …

ENTER: the number of pennies in two dollars

−	39
×	300
+	41
×	two
×	800
+	eighteen
=	

Abraham Lincoln lived in a home made of these...

ENTER: the number of dimes in a dollar

 × 600

 + seven

 − 400

= ↻

In order for one person to buy, another must…

ENTER: the number of quarters in a dollar

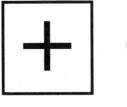 **three**

 221

 five

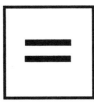 

PLACE ORDER here!

If you miss the bus, it's your...

ENTER: the cents you would have with one dime and one penny

 × five

 × 100

 + seven

 =

Your sense of direction is something you never want to…

ENTER: the number of dimes in one dollar

 **fifty**

 seven

 seven

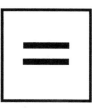 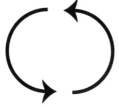

The space shuttle very quickly rocketed ___ in the sky! ...

ENTER: the number of nickels in twenty-five cents

×	896
+	(2 x 100)
-	sixty-six
=	↻

A model of the Earth is a . . .

ENTER: the number of nickels in one dollar

 .8

 thirteen

 3173

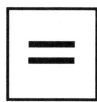 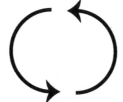

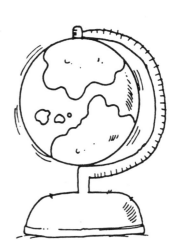

An _____ feline is another name for a fat cat! . . .

ENTER: the number of cents in five dimes

✕	4.4
✕	eight
+	nine
✕	twenty
=	↻

78

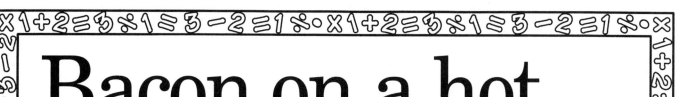

Bacon on a hot griddle might...

ENTER: the number of pennies in four dimes

$\times$ **1861**

$+$ **three**

$\times$ **five**

$=$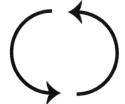

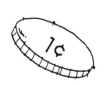

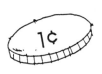

A nickname for Robert . . .

ENTER: the number of cents in a quarter and a nickel

 add (10 + 10)

 × 797

 add one

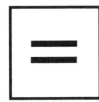 × eight

=

The ears on an African elephant are real…

ENTER: the number of pennies that equals two dimes

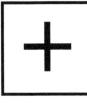 443

 one

 600

 eighteen

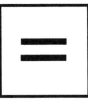 

A long-legged bird that is related to the stork and the heron…

ENTER: the number of pennies in a roll of pennies.

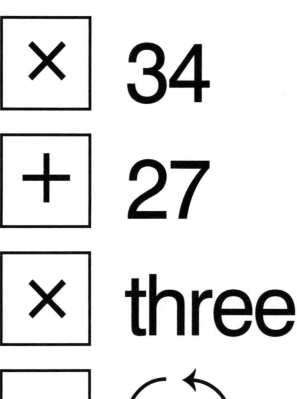

× 34

+ 27

× three

= ⟳

Which is your favorite kind of math problem?

ENTER: the number of pennies that equals four quarters

÷	two
+	one
+	.23
=	↻

Liz and Lindsey love to ride their bikes, but only Liz wears a helmet. Who is practicing good bicycle safety?...

ENTER: the number of pennies that equal a dime

 two

× ten

+ 1.217

= ⟳

A fish that looks like a snake is an…

ENTER: the number of dimes in a dollar

×	seventy
+	thirty-five
-	two
=	

What a smart person does when a skunk enters his yard…

ENTER: the amount of two quarters and three pennies

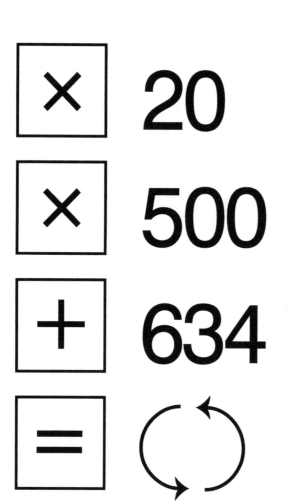

×	20
×	500
+	634
=	↻

The contraction for "I will"…

ENTER: the number of numerals on a clock face

 the number of months in two years

 twelve

 three

 12.85

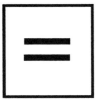 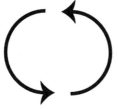

A name you might call your pet lizard...

ENTER: the first number after twelve on your clock

 **add one**

 × .11

 + .0017

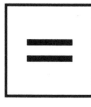 **=**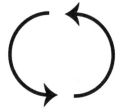

If centipedes needed these, they would go broke!...

ENTER: the number of seconds in one minute

÷	fifteen
+	one
×	10609
=	

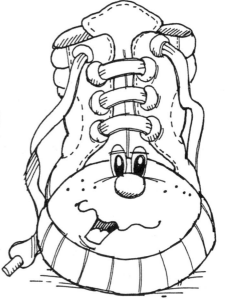

IF8361 Calculator Activities

One of America's most famous songs is "God ____ America"

ENTER: the number of seconds in one minute

 add (3 + 7)

 add (6 + 4)

–	one
×	seven hundred
+	78
=	↻

When you borrow a lot of money, you might say…

ENTER: the number of minutes in half an hour

 add (2+2+2)

 ÷ twelve

 × .03367

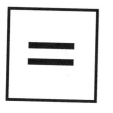 =

When it was time to move, the wagon train master shouted, "Westward…"

ENTER: the number of minutes in an hour

  the number of wheels on a wagon

  thirteen

  five

  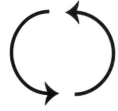

When our ice-cream cone falls on the ground, we...

ENTER: the number of hours between noon and 4 p.m.

 ×　(25+25)

 −　thirty-nine

 ×　five

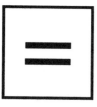 =　

This gets hurt when you're embarrassed...

ENTER: the number on a clock face that stands for fifteen minutes after the hour

 Spanish number "uno"

 five

 .07

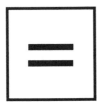 

A boy's name that rhymes with "rely"...

ENTER: the number on a clock face that stands for twenty minutes after the hour

 × **two**

 − **three**

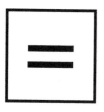 × **34.6**

 =

This means "hello" in English and "yes" in Japanese . . .

ENTER: the number on a clock face that stands for "half past the hour"

 **six**

 eight

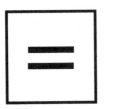 **two**

When you hear this ring, school is over…

ENTER: the number on the clock that represents five minutes before the hour

+	nineteen
×	258
−	two
=	

After the clown removed the cream pie from his face he said…

ENTER: the number of seconds in one minute, plus 7

 **multiply (5+5)**

 500

 140

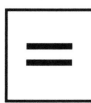 

The opposite of "she"…

ENTER: the number of days in a week

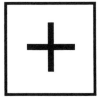 **+ eight**

 × two

 **add 2 + 2**

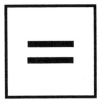 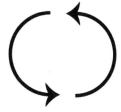

When you subtract, you always place the number with this value on the bottom…

ENTER: the number of balls used to play foursquare

 sixty-six

 seventy-nine

 244

What Saint Nicholas loves to say before "Merry Christmas"…

ENTER: the number of reindeer named Rudolph pulling Santa's sleigh

−	.79798
÷	two
×	four
=	↻

HO! HO! HO!

A turtle explaining how he moves…

ENTER: the number of days in two weeks

 two

 subtract (3+3)

 .24939

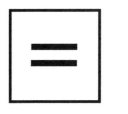 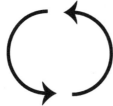

A baby might say...

ENTER: the number of people it takes to play on a seesaw

 add (3+3)

| ÷ | two |

| − | three |

| − | .93994 |

| = | ⟳ |

A beautiful instrument in the woodwind family...

ENTER: the number of holes in a bagel

 add (2+2)

× 77

× (4+4)

= ↻

A good thing to teach your dog to do...

ENTER: the number of wheels on a pair of skates

×	400
+	467
×	two
=	

My friends want to sing the high parts...

ENTER: the number of pieces you have when you cut an apple in half

 two

 .23663

 six

= ⟳

IF8361 Calculator Activities

A group of these is called a gaggle! ...

ENTER: the number of adults it takes to cook toast

 .25

 two

 4417

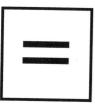 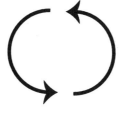

IF8361 Calculator Activities

Another name for a toucan's beak...

ENTER: the number of hands it takes to play the violin

 100

 38,593

 + eighteen

=

The tall, round structure on a farm where grain is stored...

ENTER: the number of wheels on a tractor

+	.10
+	.19
÷	six
=	

A melted candle is a ___ of wax!...

ENTER: the number of legs on a chair

 the number of prongs on a fork

 the largest group of dots on a domino

 577

The stuff farmers plant their seeds in ...

ENTER: the age at which most children start kindergarten

 add 1/2 dozen eggs

 three

 two

 203

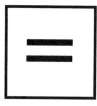 

Find the missing word in this nursery rhyme line: "Pop! _____ the weasel!" . . .

ENTER: How many blind mice there were?

➕	four
✖	two
✖	379
═	↻

When the villain enters, the audience...

ENTER: How many months old you are on your first birthday?

 divide by two

 add ten

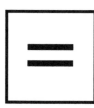 × 313

=

IF8361 Calculator Activities

The little old lady who had so many kids she didn't know what to do lived in a…

ENTER: the number of shoes that make a pair

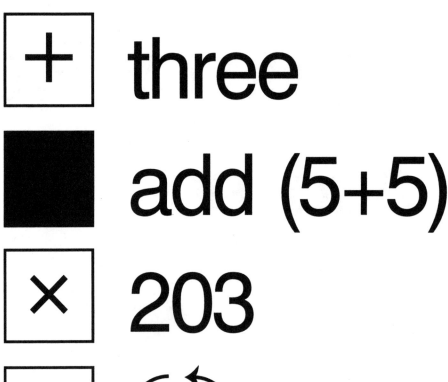

+ three

■ add (5+5)

× 203

= ↻

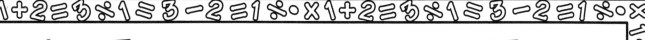

A dog can easily make a cat...

ENTER: the number of fingers you have

÷ two

+ one

× 919

= ⟳

When you sing by yourself, you sing a...

ENTER: the number of seeds in an avocado

 the number on a clock face that stands for "quarter past the hour"

 .23

 six

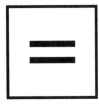 

A great tool for gardening...

ENTER: the number of toes on your left foot

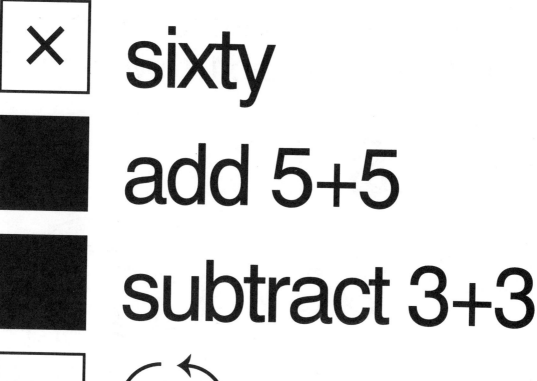

×	sixty
■	add 5+5
■	subtract 3+3
=	↻

At a green light you...

ENTER: the number of seeds in a peach

 add the number of people it takes to brush your teeth

 .8

 two

=

Add this to "zag" to describe a crooked line...

ENTER: the number of wheels on a roller skate

+	4.5
×	eight
×	nine
=	

A great device for keeping clean...

ENTER: the number of shoes in four pairs

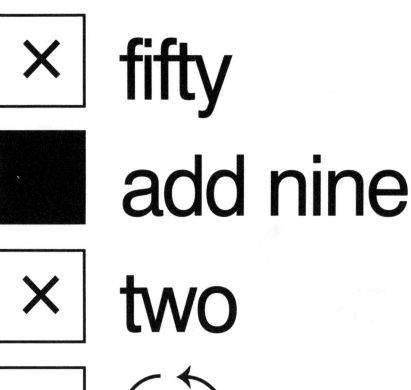

×	fifty
■	add nine
×	two
=	↻

An old-fashioned name for a spinning top...

ENTER: the number of people that can play on one hopscotch at a time

 add the greatest number: 3, 5, 2, 1, 0

 two

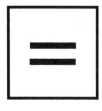 seventy-seven

The fifth tone of a musical scale is...

ENTER: the number of corners a square has

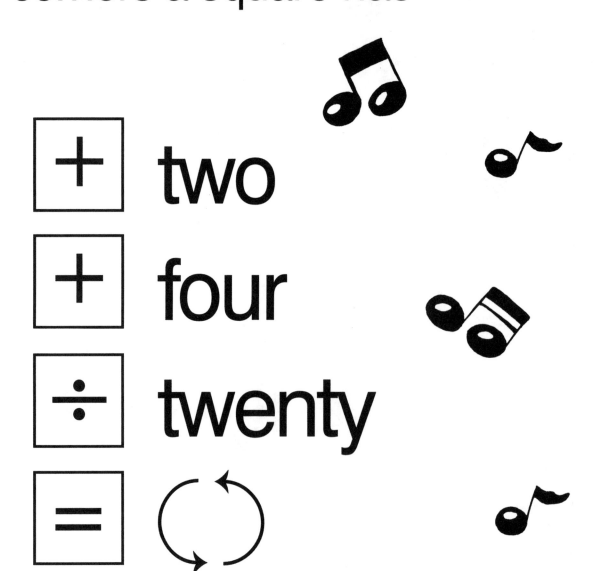

+	two
+	four
÷	twenty
=	↻

The universal distress signal ...

ENTER: the number you dial in an emergency

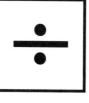 ÷ **two**

 - **.5**

 + **fifty**

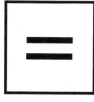 **=**

© Instructional Fair   123   IF8361 Calculator Activities

A Great Dane is very...

ENTER: the number of digits in your phone number

 one less than seventy

 three

 457

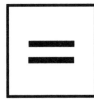 

The capital of Idaho is...

ENTER: the number of minutes in one hour

×	145
+	77
×	four
=	↻

A great name for a lion is…

ENTER: the number of push buttons on a telephone

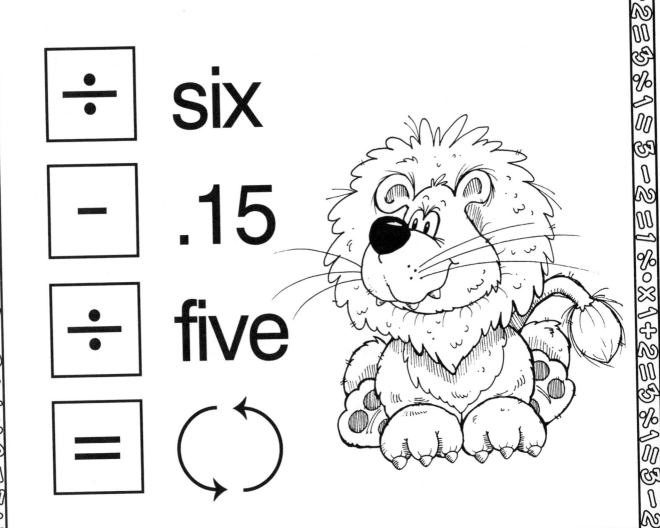

÷ six

− .15

÷ five

= ⟳

As _____ as pie...

ENTER: the number of days in a week

✕	seven
÷	two
−	1.5
=	

When you hit a tennis ball high in the air to the back of the court ...

ENTER: the largest digit on a push-button phone

 add one

 eighty

 add seven

Someone that is in the Army...

ENTER: the number of seasons throughout the year

 add the number of months in half of a year

 two

 eleven

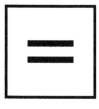 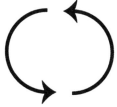

When you feel relieved you…

ENTER: the number of eggs in a dozen

×	two
+	one
×	184.6
=	↻

Where can you find elephants and penguins?...

ENTER: the number of legs on a horse + 3

$+$	ninety-three
$\div$	five
⬛	divide by 1,000
$=$	↻

The sound your boots make in the wet snow…

ENTER: the number of shoes in three pair

 × 7000

 + 3000

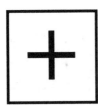 **+** the number of pennies in three quarters

 **=**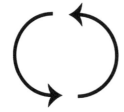

A June bug is often mistaken for a . . .

ENTER: the number of days in a school week

 80.6

 sixty

 seven

 fourteen

 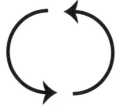

A type of Eskimo home...

ENTER: the number of corners on a square

 × **twenty-five**

 ÷ the number of pennies in a dollar

 − **.9239**

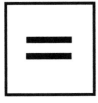 **=**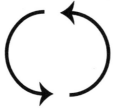

A name for a boy or girl that rhymes with see…

ENTER: the number of moons revolving around our planet

+	the number of days in the month of May
−	**twenty-six**
×	**fifty-five**
+	**seven**
=	↻

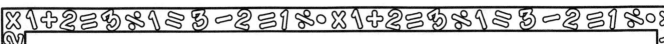

Ants work very hard to make one...

ENTER: the number of stars on the American flag

 seventy-seven

 seven

 two

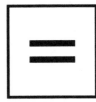 

The year both Alaska and Hawaii became part of the United States?

ENTER: the number of stripes on the American flag

+	twenty-eight
×	160
+	one
=	⟳

The fifth word in the song "The Star-Spangled Banner"…

ENTER: the number of legs on a spider

$\div$ two

$+$ one

$\times$ sixty-seven

$=$ ↻

The policeman will _____ the stolen money.

ENTER: the number of legs on an octopus

 800

 twenty-seven

 five

Something you don't want in your bicycle tire...

ENTER: the number of inches in one foot

 three

 four

 92.6

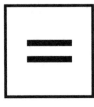 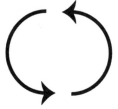

These help you see in the water. ...

ENTER: the number of ounces in one pound

$+$ 584

$\times$ 8961

$+$ six

$=$

Someone with big feet gets…

ENTER: the average normal body temperature

×	540
−	199
+	.618
=	

What you tell a fly when you want it to go away…

ENTER: the number of feet in a yard

 add the number of toes on both your feet

+ two

÷ five

− two

− .64

÷ eight

=

Who'll be comin' round the mountain when she comes?

ENTER: the day in July when we celebrate our independence

 add (7+7)

$+$ two

$+$ 444.07

$\div$ six

$=$ ↻

When we think of nursery rhymes, we think of Mother...

ENTER: the number of days in the month of January

−	**six**
×	**two**
×	**seven hundred**
■	**add six**
=	↺

Something your heart can be filled with...

ENTER: the number of days in the month of September

$\times$	one hundred
$+$	400
$-$	24
$=$	

The contraction for "he is"…

ENTER: the number of days in February in a leap year

$-$	five
$\div$	four
$\times$	.89
$=$	

A good dog shouldn't...

ENTER: the number that means "uno" in Spanish

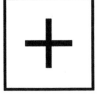 sixty-six

 two

 seven

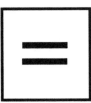 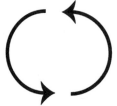

A famous bear's best friend...

ENTER: the number for the Spanish number "dos"

×	ten
-	twelve
×	.101
=	↻

What do you want to ___ when you grow up?…

ENTER: the number in most packs of hot dogs

×	four
-	twenty-four
×	4.75
=	↻

When someone is sleeping, you might hear...

ENTER YOUR RESPONSE: David and Sam are riding on their skateboards. How many wheels are turning?

−	three
×	7406
+	seven
×	six
=	

IF8361 Calculator Activities

Something that's not great is...

ENTER YOUR RESPONSE: There were six dogs at the pet talent show. One refused to walk on his hind legs. How many did?

 .0505

 two

Name for a small island...

ENTER YOUR RESPONSE: Eva and David rode their bikes over to Mark's house. Mark joined them. How many bicycle tires were there in all?

 **+** the number of eggs in two dozen

 **×** **125**

 **+** the number of tails on a kitty cat

 **=**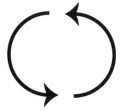

The owl is famous for making this sound...

Enter your response: Eva brought 3 apples to school. She gave 2 to her classroom teacher and one to her music teacher. How many apples did she have left?

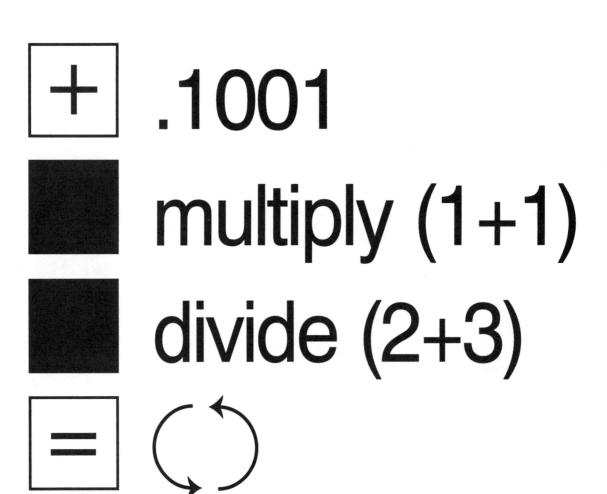

$+$ .1001

◼ multiply (1+1)

◼ divide (2+3)

$=$ ↻

Who sells sea shells at the sea shore?

ENTER YOUR RESPONSE: If kitty was given three pieces of tuna for breakfast, and for dinner, how many pieces did she have in all?

 **two**

 one before six

 twenty-three

 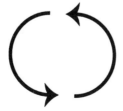

What you crack when you want to scramble...

ENTER YOUR RESPONSE: There were five carrots in Monica's lunch bag. She ate two, and gave one away. How many did she have left over to munch on after school?

 add three

 160

 nine

 seven

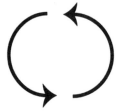 

I want a big hug or...

ENTER YOUR RESPONSE: Your pet Mittens had five kittens. How many tiny paws are scrambling over your kitchen floor?

□ −	ten
□ ×	four hundred
□ −	427
□ =	⟳

Very hot water might…

ENTER YOUR RESPONSE: Mandi cooked three ears of corn. She broke each of them in half. How many pieces of corn did she have altogether?

 **ten**

 **two**

 **888.5**

IF8361 Calculator Activities

This girl's name begins with an "L"...

ENTER YOUR RESPONSE: Steven earned $2.00 baby-sitting his neighbor's kitty! He also earned $2.00 for doing his chores. How much more will he need to get a total of $5.00?

 add 49

 102

 seven

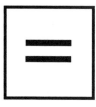 

Answer Key

1. Big Hog (604618)
2. EBGBs (5.8683)
3. Bibless (5537818)
4. Boogie (316008)
5. Belle (37738)
6. Gills (57716)
7. Hobbies (5318804)
8. Globless (55378076)
9. Eloise (351073)
10. Egg Shell (77345663)
11. Bliss (55178)
12. Bibble (378818)
13. Big Logs (5607618)
14. Loose (35007)
15. Biggie (316618)
16. Bill (7718)
17. Shoebill (77183045)
18. Legible (3781637)
19. Big Bib (818618)
20. Beeless (5537338)
21. Gloss (55076)
22. Goose Egg (66335006)
23. Boo Boos (5008008)
24. Ssssssss (55555555)
25. Ill (771)
26. Shells (577345)
27. Giggle (376616)
28. Lilies (53717)
29. Billie (317718)
30. Bobble (378808)
31. Logo (0.067)
32. Seis (5135)
33. Sill (7715)
34. She's (5.345)
35. Gobs (5806)
36. Liz (217)
37. Eh (43)
38. Ozzie (31220)
29. Sillies (5317715)
40. Hee Hee (334334)
41. Gib (816)
42. Gobble (318806)
43. Bible (37818)
44. Size (3215)
45. Sleigh (461375)
46. Bellies (5317738)
47. Leslie (317537)
48. Boggles (5376608)
49. Bo (0.8)
50. Oso (0.50)
51. Hobble (378804)
52. Oh (40)
53. E I E I O (0.1313)

54. Hose (3504)
55. Beige (36138)
56. I (1)
57. Oozes (53200)
58. Ohio (0.140)
59. Bob (808)
60. Gee (336)
61. Boo Hoo (0.04008)
62. Oil (710)
63. Lie (317)
64. Sole (3705)
65. Gil (716)
66. Sis (515)
67. Boss (5508)
68. Bees (5338)
69. Hello (0.7734)
70. Hog (604)
71. Big Shell (77345618)
72. Logs (5607)
73. Sell (7735)
74. Loss (5507)
75. Lose (3507)
76. High (4614)
77. Globe (38076)
78. Obese (35380)
79. Sizzle (372215)
80. Bobbie (318808)
81. Biggies (5316618)
82. Ibis (5181)
83. Ez Is (51.23)
84. Liz Is (51.217)
85. Eel (733)
86. He Goes (530634)
87. I'll (77.1)
88. Lizzo (0.2217)
89. Shoes (53045)
90. Bless (55378)
91. IO IO IO (0.10101)
92. Ho (0.4)
93. Sob (508)
94. Ego (0.63)
95. Eli (173)
96. Hi (14)
97. Bell (7738)
98. Oh I See (335140)
99. He (34)
100. Less (5537)
101. Ho Ho Ho (0.40404)
102. I Go Slo (0.75061)
103. Goo Goo (0.06006)
104. Oboe (3080)
105. Heel (7334)
106. So I Go Lo (0.706105)

107. Geese (35336)
108. Big Bill (7718618)
109. Silo (0.715)
110. Blob (8078)
111. Soil (71-5)
112. Goes (5306)
113. Boos (5008)
114. Shoe (3045)
115. Hiss (5514)
116. Solo (0.705)
117. Hoe (304)
118. Go (0.6)
119. Zig (612)
120. Bib (818)
121. Gig (616)
122. So (0.5)
123. SOS (505)
124. Big (618)
125. Boise (35108)
126. Leo (0.37)
127. Ez (23)
128. Lob (807)
129. GI (16)
130. Sigh (4615)
131. Zoo (0.02)
132. Slosh (45075)
133. Big Bee (338618)
134. Igloo (0.0761)
135. Lee (337)
136. Hill (7714)
137. 1959 (6561)
138. See (335)
139. Seize (32135)
140. Hole (3704)
141. Goggles (5376606)
142. Big Shoes (53045.618)
143. Shoo (0.045)
144. She'll (77.345)
145. Goose (35006)
146. Glee (3376)
147. He's (5.34)
148. Beg (938)
149. Bo Bo (0.808)
150. Be (38)
151. Zzzzzz (222222)
152. So So (0.505)·
153. Isle (3751)
154. Hoo Hoo (0.04004)
155. She (345)
156. Eggs (5663)
157. Else (3573)
158. Boil (7108)
159. Lois (5107)

IF8361 Calculator Activities